Loo-Loo, Boo, and Art You Can Do

by Denis Roche

Houghton Mifflin Company

Boston 1996

For information about this and other Houghton Mifflin
trade and reference books and multimedia products,
visit The Bookstore at Houghton Mifflin on the World
Wide Web at http://www.hmco.com/trade/.

Manufactured in Singapore

Typography by David Saylor and Ariel Apte.
The text of this book is set in 13 point Univers Bold.
The illustrations are gouache, reproduced in full color.

TWP 10 9 8 7 6 5 4 3 2 1

LIBRARY OF CONGRESS CATALOGING-IN-PUBLICATION DATA
Roche, Denis.
Loo-Loo, Boo and art you can do / Denis Roche.
p. cm.
Summary: Presents instructions for a variety of simple art projects,
including painting, potato prints, face masks, collage, papier mache,
and clay beads.
ISBN 0-395-75921-8
1. Handicraft– Juvenile literature. {1. Handicraft.}
I. Title.   TT160.r577   1996   704'.544–dc20
95-21971   CIP   AC

Tables of Content

I'm Loo-Loo and that's Boo. This is a book of some of our favorite art projects that you can make too. You don't have to do these projects in order—pick any one and then follow us. We hope that you enjoy these projects as much as we do!
The art you create isn't going to look like anyone else's because, after all, do you look exactly like anyone else? The art you make will always be wonderful because it is a reflection of you!

Stuff We Need To Tell You Before You Begin

You might want to wear a smock when you paint or do other messy projects. Get an old T-shirt or shirt from your parent and wear that. Some people like to wear their smocks backward so that paint and goo doesn't fall through the buttonholes. Don't forget to roll up your sleeves!

You can do any project on the floor or on a table. Usually it is a good idea to lay down newspapers before you start. Water jars and paint almost always tip over, and it's easier to clean up if you've put down newspapers. You can tape the newspapers down to make them less slippery.

What kind of glue should you use? Glue sticks are OK for paper, but we think white liquid glue works best for the projects in this book.

Help!

You're so strong!

There are two kinds of paint you can use. Watercolor paint is a thin paint. It shows up best on white paper. Watercolor paint will have <u>more</u> color if you use <u>less</u> water.

Poster paint is also called tempera paint. This paint is very thick and lots of fun to use. Poster paint is good for mixing new colors or working on cardboard. It usually doesn't wash out of clothing.

If your paint came in big jars, it is easier to use and share if you pour smaller amounts into an empty egg carton. You can use the extra spaces in the carton to mix new colors. Some people like to use plates (paper or real) to mix colors too.

While you're painting, you need a water jar so you can clean your brush every time you change colors. Use a bigger water jar for bigger brushes and change your water when it gets really yucky. When you're finished painting, wash your brushes in the sink until all the paint stuck on them goes down the drain.

Potato Prints

(Potato-head)

A print is a mark or design that can be repeated over and over and over again. If you step in mud, your shoe will print that mud in a shoe print over and over until your mom tells you to take off your shoes. Using potatoes and paint, you'll be able to make prints on paper.

Ask your parents for whole, uncooked potatoes. They probably keep them in the kitchen.

Cut the potatoes in half with a plastic knife, then put the flat part of the potato on the table.

Now here comes the tricky part.

(But any potato-head can do it.)

Looking down at your potato half, you see a circle. You need to cut the edges off the potato to make different shapes.

Can you make a square? Using your knife, cut off pieces of the circle to make one.

A star?

What other shapes can you make?

Now you're going to print. Pour poster paint onto a plate. Press the face of the potato into the paint, then press it down on a piece of paper. You can print more than one time before you need to dip the potato back into the paint again.

When you're finished printing and waiting for the paint to dry, try balancing a whole potato on your head.

Sculptures

Have you ever pretended that you were a statue? A statue is a sculpture. A sculpture is a piece of art that has more than one side. A sculpture is never flat.

To make your sculpture you'll need:

a flat piece of cardboard

empty cans

empty milk cartons

cardboard tubes

any kind of boxes

glue

Where do you get cardboard tubes? From paper towels and toilet paper, of course. But wait until the paper is finished before you use them!

Wash any dirty cans or cartons.

What you decide to build can look like anything or nothing at all. Sometimes the shape of your cans and cartons will give you ideas.

Use the flat piece of cardboard as a base for your sculpture. Build up from the piece of cardboard, using the cans, milk cartons, and tubes, gluing them together as you go along.

When you're done building, you can paint or decorate your sculpture.

Bumpy Paint

It's important for roads to be flat.

And flat toast is a good idea too, because then you can spread stuff on it easily.

But do paintings have to be flat?

There's really no good reason.

Here's a way to make a bumpy painting.

You'll need:

empty cans or jars

sand

poster paint

glue

big paintbrushes

paper

Put some sand into each of your cans or jars.

Now pour the same amount of paint into each one.

Add a big squirt of glue to each jar.

With big paintbrushes, stir the mixtures until they're as thick as milk shakes.

It's going to feel different painting with bumpy paint. You smush it onto the paper instead of smoothing it on.

When you're finished painting and ready to clean up, do not put any paint down the sink. Throw it in the trash instead, and wash your brushes extra well.

Stinky Clay

There are lots of things you can make with clay, and even more things to make if you change your mind.

Stinky clay is a really smelly clay-dough. Each time you're finished playing with it, put it in something with a tight top. A coffee can will work well, or a plastic bag tied shut.

You'll need these things to make stinky clay:

A big bowl

3 tablespoons of baking powder

1/2 cup of pickle juice or vinegar

1 cup of flour

1 tablespoon of vegetable oil

X-TRA UGLY.

food coloring or poster paint (any yucky color will do)

Put the 3 tablespoons of baking powder into a bowl.

Now add 1/2 cup of pickle juice (without the pickles!) or vinegar. Don't worry, it's supposed to fizz!

Mix in 1 cup of flour and 1 tablespoon of oil. Smush the bumps with your fingers.

Last of all, add a few drops of food coloring or paint. If your mixture is too dry, add water. If it is too wet, add a little bit of flour. Mix well, until it's really stinky.

Is your clay stinky enough? Probably!

A lot of people are scared of stinky clay, but don't let this stop you from playing with it!

Face Masks

You can wear a mask anytime you want to hide your face. Some masks are scary.

Some masks are silly. My grandma even has a special mask to wear at night.

To make your mask, you need a piece of cardboard large enough to at least cover your eyes. Use your fingers to measure how far apart your eyes are. Mark this distance on your cardboard.

Hold the piece of cardboard in your hands and use scissors to make eye holes.

Can you see?

You can cut your mask . . .

in any shape.

How is your mask going to stay on? Staple a piece of string — knotted at the ends — to each side of your mask, and then tie these in the back to keep your mask on.

Use glue to add anything to your mask. All of these things make good noses.

GLUE

a button

a cardboard tube

macaroni

Hair can be made from anything too.

pipe cleaners

cut paper

yarn

socks

What else?

Don't forget to paint your mask when you're finished (but take it off first!).

Crayon Magic

Crayons smell great and are terrific for coloring and drawing.

But did you know that you can write and draw magic messages with crayons?

Using a WHITE crayon, write or draw your magic message on a WHITE piece of paper.

Give your piece of paper to a friend. If they paint the piece of paper with watercolor paint...

VOILÀ!
Your secret message will appear.

You can also trace things with crayons. To do this, you need to peel the paper off your crayon like you peel the skin off a banana.

Now find an object or a surface that is hard and bumpy.

Place your paper on top of that surface.

Rub the paper with the long side of your crayon until your tracing appears. Try tracing coins, the bottom of your shoes . . . what else?

You can cut out anything that you think looks interesting.

Sometimes a collage can be about an idea.

When you're tired of cutting and tearing, you can begin to glue. You can glue your pieces onto the paper side by side . . .

or overlapping each other.

You might even want to paint or draw over your collage when you're finished.

Hats

One of the best things about having a head is that you can easily wear hats. There are many different kinds of hats in the world. Sometimes a hat can tell you about the person who is wearing it. Can you make a hat that tells us about you?

First you need to measure around your head with a piece of string. Make a mark where the string touches itself so you know how big your head is.
Cut the string at the mark.

Now find a piece of cardboard a little longer than the piece of string. The cardboard can be as tall or short as you want it to be; really, all that matters is that it is long enough to fit around your head.

Slowly bend the cardboard by rolling it around a bottle the long way. Now your hat will fit you better.

Put on your hat. Is it too tall? No problem — take off your hat and lay it flat again. Using scissors, cut straight across to make it shorter, or cut zigzags, waves, or bumps to make it shorter and weirder.

Now glue or staple your hat together.

You can color your hat and add anything to it. Since this hat tells the world something about you, you'll know best how to decorate it!

Papier-Mâché

Papier-Mâché is another way to make sculpture. This is one of the gooiest projects we know. You'll look like this when you're finished. Wear old clothes or a smock.

Gather your materials first. You'll need:

newspapers

maybe balloons

tape

a big bowl

2 cups of flour

3 cups of water

glue

Now you're going to make the form or shape of your sculpture. This can be done by crumpling up newspaper into balls and taping them together. You can also tape balloons together to make a form.

Take the leftover newspapers and rip them into strips as wide as your arm.

Pour 2 cups of flour into the bowl. Mix in 3 cups of water and a big squirt of glue, and stir with your hands. Smush the lumps with your fingers until the goo mixture is smooth. It should be as thick as a milk shake at the end. Add more water or flour if you need to.

Dip the strips into the goo-bowl one at a time, and begin wrapping them around your form.

To make your sculpture really strong, wrap the strips in different directions. Make about three layers of strips. If it all gets too soggy, let your sculpture dry a couple of hours before continuing.

Once you've finished wrapping your form, spread a little extra goo all over the sculpture with your hand. Your sculpture will take at least a day to dry completely. Once it is dry, you can decorate it with paint, beads, or anything else you like.

Make Another You!

You're pretty amazing, so why shouldn't there be two of you? Or four?

To make another you, you'll need two really big pieces of paper. Each should be big enough so that all of you can fit on it when you lie down.

Lie down on the paper and choose your position. Can you look like you're swimming? Running? Now have a friend trace your outline with a crayon. Stay still!

If you get ticklish . . .

begin again.

Cut out your shape, and place this on the second large piece of paper.

Hold your cut-out piece with one paw and trace around its edges. Now you've drawn yourself again on the second piece of paper.

Cut yourself out again.

Put the two pieces together and start stapling around the edges.

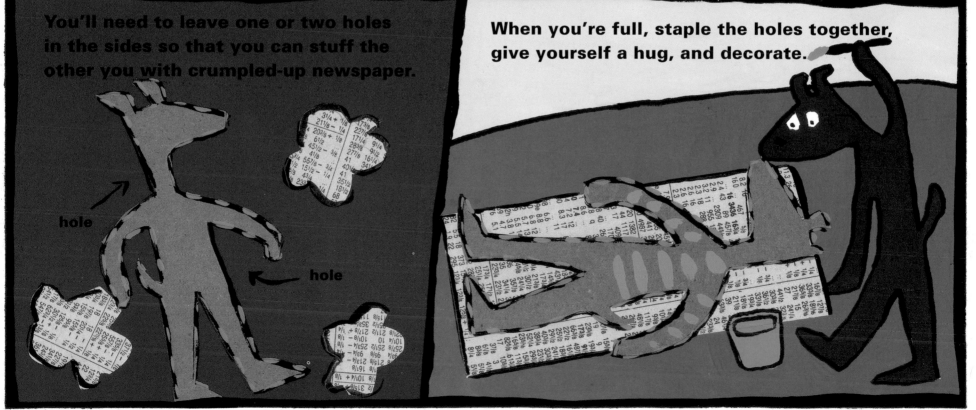

You'll need to leave one or two holes in the sides so that you can stuff the other you with crumpled-up newspaper.

hole

hole

When you're full, staple the holes together, give yourself a hug, and decorate.

Clay Beads

Have you ever noticed what happens to clay when you forget to put it away?

It gets hard.

Hello!

Where have you been?

Here's a recipe for a kind of clay that's supposed to get hard after you shape it. Once it's hard and dry, you can paint it.

You'll need:

a big bowl

1 cup of flour

1 cup of salt

1 heaping teaspoon of cornstarch or baking powder

water, but no fish please!

pencil

poster paint

brush

clear nail polish

string

In the big bowl, mix 1 cup of flour, 1 cup of salt, and one heaping teaspoon of cornstarch (or baking powder). Then add water, one drop at a time. If you add too much water, it will feel like mud, and then it will be too wet to shape.

too much water

just right

If your clay is too wet, try adding more salt, flour, and cornstarch to make it drier. If it is too dry, add a teeny bit of water. Once the mixture feels smushy and not crumbly or gooey, you're ready to make beads.

Let's go!

To make a round bead, pinch off a piece of clay and put it in the palm of your paw. Roll it around in a circle until it becomes a ball. Now try to make a square-shaped bead or a heart-shaped bead.

Make enough beads for a necklace. Poke a hole through the center of each bead with a pencil. The hole needs to go all the way through the bead.

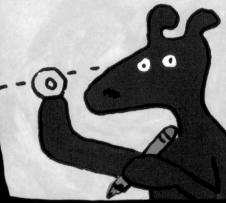

The beads now need time to dry. They may take up to two whole days to dry.

Go back to sleep!

We're not ready yet!

When the beads are hard and dry, you can paint them with poster paint. Make sure the paint doesn't block the bead's hole. To be extra fancy, paint your beads with clear nail polish once the poster paint has dried. This will make them shiny.

String your beads and wear them out to dinner. People will be amazed by how beautiful they are!

31

We had fun making art with you, and don't forget that you can do these projects over and over again. See you later!
Congratulations! You made some amazing art. Did you know that you were such a wonderful artist? We did. Please close this book carefully so you don't smush us. Good-bye!
FLOUR
XXX